The
ROYAL CORPS
of SIGNALS

A PICTORIAL HISTORY

SPECIAL EDITION MARKING THE 25TH ANNIVERSARY
OF HRH THE PRINCESS ROYAL AS COLONEL IN CHIEF
OF THE ROYAL CORPS OF SIGNALS

A proportion of the proceeds of each copy will go to the
Royal Signals Benevolent Association.

Her Royal Highness The Princess Royal
Princess Mary
(Our first Colonel in Chief)

Her Royal Highness The Princess Royal
(Our present Colonel in Chief)

The Colonels in Chief of the Royal Corps of Signals.

The
ROYAL CORPS
of SIGNALS

A PICTORIAL HISTORY

Laurette Burton

TEMPUS

First published 2002
Copyright © Laurette Burton, 2002

Tempus Publishing Limited
The Mill, Brimscombe Port,
Stroud, Gloucestershire, GL5 2QG

ISBN 0 7524 2391 6

Typesetting and origination by
Tempus Publishing Limited
Printed in Great Britain by
Midway Colour Print, Wiltshire

The Corps Memorial, Blandford Camp.

Contents

Members of the Telegraph Battalion at Chevening Camp in 1891. Standing from left to right: Lieutenant (later Brigadier-General) E.G. Godfrey Faussett, Lieutenant C.J. Elkington, Surgeon Captain Hardy and Captain W.F. Hawkins. Seated from left to right: Lieutenant R.H.H. Boys, Captain C.F.C. Beresford, Lieutenant J.S. Fowler (later Lieutenant General Sir) and Captain F.G. Bowles. It was at the suggestion of Captain (later Major) Beresford that Mercury became the emblem for Signallers and the badge he designed is clearly visible above the opening to the tent. Lieutenant Fowler was to become first Colonel Commandant of the Royal Corps of Signals and Lieutenant Godfrey Faussett first Commandant of the Signal Training Centre at Maresfield Park in Sussex.

Introduction

This collection of photographs is neither a definitive history of the Royal Corps of Signals nor a history of military signalling. Rather its intention is to provide an outline of the heritage of the Corps and an impression of its involvement in the historic events which have charted the nation's history over the past century and more. It touches upon invention and innovation, exploration and operations, and the character and courage of the many thousands who have served in the Corps and its antecedents. In particular it aims to illustrate the ubiquity of signallers: 'first in, last out' in every operation, on every continent and in every military environment from airborne to armour and from static tasks to special forces.

The provision of the right information to the right place at the right time has always been crucial to the successful conduct of war. For thousands of years runners and dispatch riders were the mainstay of communication on the battlefield, epitomized by the Greek Pheidipiddes and his epic run to carry news of the battle of Marathon. Twenty-two centuries ago the Carthaginians used torches as an early form of signalling lamp and, in battles between the Greeks and Persians, a polished shield was employed as the first rather crude form of heliograph. Signalling with flags and smoke and the use of carrier pigeons to convey messages also have origins in the earliest times.

The larger, better equipped and more mobile armies of the nineteenth century necessitated more rapid methods of sending messages over longer distances. Developments in the Industrial Revolution were to answer these requirements and heralded momentous changes in communications both for war and peace. Two major innovations were semaphore and the electric telegraph. Semaphore signalling had started in the late eighteenth century and by 1816 messages were being conveyed from London to Portsmouth and other posts by a system of shutters placed on towers on hills – the shutter telegraph. However, the system had its disadvantages particularly in bad weather when transmissions were interrupted by fog or mist.

The electric telegraph was to prove a more efficient method of communication. Although Galileo, the seventeenth-century astronomer, had thought it possible to converse at great distances using magnetic needles, the telegraph did not become a practical reality until about 1835. Telegraph was used for the first time in war in the Crimea and shortly afterwards the Royal Engineers took over responsibility for telegraphic work. It is at this point that the story of the Royal Corps of Signals begins.

All technological developments in communications have had but one aim, to secure success in military operations, and it is on these operations that signallers have proved their mettle both as soldiers and as tradesmen. The Corps has been fortunate to attract people of ability with wide interests and expertise. It has produced many sportsmen of international renown from Geoff Duke, World Champion motorcyclist, to Kriss Akabusi, Olympic athlete. Explorers and mountaineers such as Bagnold, Burridge and Meikelejohn and heroes like Signalman Smith GC are just some among a wealth of selfless individuals and stalwarts who have quietly gone on their way having made a contribution to their community and comrades.

This book does not tell all their stories but I hope that it will provoke interest in their exploits as well as providing a greater understanding of the achievements of the Corps during its short history. At the dawn of the 'information age' signallers are faced with great opportunity.

Whilst the future cannot be foretold by a study of the past, the history of the Corps is characterised by innovation and tenacity as well as easy comradeship borne of mutual respect for professional skill. These characteristics will continue to be as valuable as they have been throughout Corps history to ensure that communications remain always 'Swift and Sure'.

ACKNOWLEDGEMENTS

Without the help and support of many people associated with the Corps I could not have completed this book. In particular, I would like to thank Colonel Cliff Walters, Mr Adam Forty, Stella McIntyre and Mr Tim Stankus, all of the Royal Signals Museum. Also, Lieutenant Colonel Fred Orr OBE, Lieutenant Colonel Peter Richards, Brigadier Noel Moss, Brigadier John Almonds, Major Peter Unwin, Major Richard Hoghton, WOI (CRSM) S. Keilty, Major James Anderson, Lieutenant Colonel Paul Vingoe and Mr and Mrs Len Manning. Not least I must mention my husband, Brigadier Cedric Burton OBE ADC, whose technical advice and moral support were much appreciated.

Very special thanks must go to Jane Stockdale to whom I am indebted for the major contribution she made to the project helping both in the collection of photographs and research. Without her tremendous efforts the material would never had reached the publishers on time.

Finally, my thanks to Andy and Sue Parlour who gave permission for me to use a photograph from their book *Phantom at War*.

One
From 1870 to 1919

Captain Montague Lambert, first Commander of 'C' Telegraph Troop Royal Engineers. The Troop, formed in 1870, was the earliest formal professional body of Army signallers and direct ancestor of the Royal Corps of Signals. Its duty was to provide communications for the field army by means of visual signalling, mounted orderlies and telegraph, so linking the expeditionary force into the growing worldwide telegraph network. In 1882 Sir Garnet Wolesley ordered the Troop to telegraph news of his victory over Arabi Pasha in Egypt to Queen Victoria in Balmoral. The Queen's response was received in less than an hour.

A Wire Wagon of 'C' Telegraph Troop. Two officers and 133 soldiers staffed 'C' Troop in its first year of existence and it was equipped with twelve four-wheeled, horse-drawn wire wagons. Nine of these wagons were fitted with six drums of half a mile of heavy, three-stranded cable, the other three carried seven drums. In addition there were four wagons fitted with instruments, six that transported the stores and one designed as a pontoon. By 1871 the Troop's complement had increased to five officers and 245 other ranks.

'C' Telegraph Troop at Blandford in 1872. The Troop was taking part in large-scale manoeuvres in the South of England and was camped on the old Blandford Race Course. The Race Course had been the site of a Shutter Relay Station of the type designed by the Rev. Lord George Murray in the early part of the nineteenth century. Appropriately, this area now forms a part of Blandford Camp, the present home of the Royal Corps of Signals.

Major A.C. Hamilton (later 10th Lord Belhaven and Stenton). In 1879 Major Hamilton embarked with half of ' C' Troop for the Zulu Wars, providing the Troop with its first taste of war. In spite of malaria, veldt fires and swollen rivers, the Troop succeeded in laying a large amount of air-line and cable. The heliograph, which came into service with the British and Indian Armies in about 1875, was used successfully for the first time on operations in this campaign. It used an oscillating mirror to reflect sunlight and send morse signals over long distances at speeds of sixteen words a minute. Ranges of up to 100 miles could be achieved but only in fair weather.

Lieutenant *Sir R.W. Anstruther Bt and Lieutenant G.M. Heath with No.1 Section in Bechuanaland 1885*. In 1884 'C' Troop was amalgamated with two other Royal Engineers Companies to form the Telegraph Battalion. No.1 Section was mobilised in late 1884 to assist in the task of reinstating the natives of Bechuanaland on their lands. Ahead of the main body the Section laid 350 miles of air-line at an average rate of six miles a day in very difficult terrain. This was the first test of the new air-line equipment which proved very satisfactory.

A group of soldiers at the School of Signalling, Aldershot in 1893. Formal training in both electrical and visual methods of signalling started at the School of Military Engineering in Chatham in 1869 under an Instructor of Telegraphy and an Instructor of Army Signalling. Six years later the Instructor of Army Signalling moved to Aldershot causing a division in training responsibilities between visual methods operated by all arms and line telegraphy operated by Sappers only.

The Band of the Telegraph Battalion with Lieutenant Elkington Royal Engineers, seated centre in 1891. Corporal Cork, acting Drum Major, holds the Mercury-topped mace presented to the Band by Lieutenant Elkington and Major Beresford. This same mace is now on display in the Royal Signals Museum in Blandford.

Royal Engineers Telegraph Staff in Hong Kong in 1897. After the defeat of China in the Opium War of 1839-1842, Britain acquired Hong Kong Island and, from 1860, dominated China's commerce. This lucrative trade was threatened in the latter part of the century when, sensing China's weakness, Russia, Germany and France bid for territory and a share of trade. To bolster her influence Britain leased the New Territories on the mainland adjacent to Hong Kong and reinforced her naval and military bases in the area.

Lanark Volunteers (later 52nd Lowland Signal Regiment and now 33rd (Scottish) Signal Regiment) at Chatham in 1899 en route for the South African War. Fourteen years of peace interrupted only by the second Ashanti War of 1895 gave telegraph troops time for training that, coupled with experience gained in earlier conflicts such as Egypt, Bechuanaland and Suakin, was to be of great value in the South African campaign.

Ground to air communications via balloon during the siege of Ladysmith in late 1899. Headquarters and No.1 Section of the 1st Telegraph Division left England for Natal and did admirable work in assisting the small garrison of Ladysmith to hold the large circuit of defence lines. During the siege Sir George White, Commander of the garrison, directed his artillery fire using the observation balloon which was connected to the telephone exchange.

A cable laying cycle in the Boer War. A variety of innovative ideas for assisting the provision of telegraph lines were tried as the demand for communications increased. A limited use of telephones was made in the South African War but it was sometime before the Army accepted this new technology.

By the end of the war twenty-four officers and 2424 men were engaged in telegraph work and some 3.5 million messages had been sent. Telegraphs were now seen as indispensable to a modern army for tactical purposes. But visual work and telegraphy remained separate entities with Directors for each area. When, on 1 October 1910, Telegraphs were re-named Signals this confusion and lack of economy ceased.

The first mobile Wireless Station, the Thorneycroft Steam Omnibus in 1901. Guiglielmo Marconi, father of wireless communications, is standing on the right and Professor Ambrose Fleming, inventor of the wireless valve is seated on the rear steps of the vehicle. The Marconi Wireless Telegraph Company installed a wireless set in the omnibus designed to meet the military specification of a twenty-mile range with security from enemy interference within two miles. However, Army trials highlighted the vehicle's shortcomings; it burned coal which was bulky and could only carry fuel for forty miles. It was soon replaced by a petrol-driven version.

An Adjutants' Signalling Course, Landour, India, 1908. Military Signalling in India developed in parallel with the British Army. Prior to 1911 signalling arrangements were ad hoc with no specific organisation responsible for the task. Subsequently a Signal Service was created in the form of Signal Companies of Sappers and Miners. This was implemented under proposals developed by Lord Kitchener Commander in Chief India, who had once been Adjutant of 'C' Telegraph Troop.

Wireless Carts in use by the Territorial Army in 1908. It is interesting to note the sophisticated telescopic masts that are not unlike the masts in use with the Corps today. The trials' wirelesses were large and cumbersome and could only transmit long waves and the receivers lacked sensitivity and selectivity. The development of thermionic valves, the diode in 1904 and the triode in 1907, resulted in both substantial increases in power output and the design of more compact and mobile radios.

The instrument section of a Wireless Cart in 1910 with Company Sergeant Major 'Derby' Wright in earphones on the right. This early radio set, known as 'wireless', was a 3kW transmitter with a wavelength of eighty feet. The newly formed Wireless Company was attached to the Cavalry Division to support their more mobile role.

The Royal Engineers Cycle Section and horses of the 2nd Division of the Telegraph Battalion at Rowlands Castle in 1910. The cyclists are carrying signalling flags. Assistant Surgeon A.J. Myer of the US Army developed flag signalling, known as 'wig wag', in 1835. It was used extensively until the beginning of the Second World War and was the preferred method of visual signalling in mountains and by the cavalry since flags were easier to carry than either heliograph or lamps.

A Northern Telegraph Company Detachment Royal Engineers, erecting air-line near Boston Spa, 1909. Air-line equipment designed for field telegraphy was carried in wagons and, in average English country, air-line could be erected at a pace of not less than one mile per hour. A detachment could put up at least five miles of line in the course of an average day's march and three or four detachments were thus able to place the headquarters of a force, including infantry, in communications with base at the end of every day's march (twenty to twenty-five miles).

Sapper Reg Biart (in earphones) with fellow soldiers of 'K' Company Royal Engineers in Southern Ireland, c.1912. 'K' Company Royal Engineers was formed from 2nd Division Telegraph Battalion, previously the 34th Company Royal Engineers, which provided trained men and expertise to the newly privatised General Post Office in 1870. By 1909 GPO practice in England was no longer relevant to the methods in use in the field army and 'K' Company moved to Southern Ireland. The cable wagon shown was of the type issued to the Army in 1905. Designed by Lieutenant (later Colonel Sir Harry Mackworth CMG DSO) Mackworth during the South African War, it proved a lot lighter and more manoeuvrable than its predecessor, the cable cart.

Royal Engineers Southern England Army Telegraph Section 'Why should England tremble?' c.1912. In the years between the turn of the century and 1914 there was an increasing realisation that a major struggle for power in Europe was inevitable. This light-hearted picture illustrates an attempt by some members of the Royal Engineers Signal Service to raise spirits!

1 Company, Divisional Signals, Wireless Telegraphy Detachment, 1914. Mounted at the front of the picture, from left to right: Sappers Grigg, Ball, Donovan, McGregor and Elsmore. The Elsmore family had a long tradition of service in Signals. Sapper (later Lieutenant Colonel) Elsmore's father, Corporal Elsmore proved a hero in the Egyptian campaign of 1882, the culminating action of which was a five mile night advance to the enemy's well-fortified position. Corporal Elsmore was tasked with erecting signal poles for two miles through hostile territory in the dark. Once this feat had been accomplished Elsmore and a comrade lead the advancing column, navigating by the stars and laying cable at the same time.

A Cable Section crossing a temporary bridge during the counter-attack on the River Marne, September 1914. In August 1914 Germany invaded Belgium and Britain went to war. The British Expeditionary Force (BEF) was despatched to France and deployed on the left of the Allied line. In the initial German offensive the BEF put up a fierce fight at Mons but, under attack by immeasurably superior numbers, had to pull back. During the retreat the Signals proved extremely resourceful, using civil lines to maintain communication wherever possible and eventually linking up all brigades by laying cable at the canter. The German offensive broke at the Marne, their army was driven back to the Aisne and the threat to Paris averted.

Corporal Hurlston, a Despatch Rider, with a Germany Calvary Officer's satchel for a souvenir, 1914. The Motor-Cycle Despatch Rider Service was established in 1912 and Despatch Riders were soon in action in the War distinguishing themselves by their ability to take messages where telegraph lines had been destroyed or roads damaged or blocked. They were obvious targets for snipers and casualty rates were high. In March 1918 the Despatch Riders of the 42nd Divisional Signal Company were the only remaining means of communication in the face of the German advance. In recognition of their most gallant and untiring efforts they were awarded four Military Medals in one day.

Mr Raoul Edwards, 1914. Many volunteers for despatch duties were wealthy individuals who could provide their own transport. Mr Edwards, a South American, was one of two men who drove their own Rolls-Royce cars.

Sapper (later Sergeant) W. Geddes – Despatch Rider with 14th Signal Company Royal Engineers at Ypres.

A group of Royal Engineers Telegraphists, Linemen and Despatch Riders with French interpreters at Amiens, August 1914. Note the arm-bands worn by the Despatch Riders. These blue and white bands were introduced at the beginning of the First World War to enable all members of the Signal Service to have free access across the battlefield and subsequently throughout the trench system. This distinctive device continued in use throughout the 1920s, 1930s and the Second World War, and was only removed from service in 1961.

Dog laying cable – 1914/1918. Dogs were trained to carry cable dispensers on their backs and could lay cable over short distances. They could also deliver messages, moving three times faster than a man whilst providing less of a target for the enemy. Stories of their heroism abound and many battled on when badly gassed or wounded. A post mortem on one dog revealed that he had been carrying messages for weeks with a bullet in his lungs and a piece of shrapnel in his spine.

Motorcyclists preparing to deliver birds of the Carrier Pigeon Service to outstations. The carrier pigeon had for hundreds of years proved a dependable and speedy means of conveying messages on the battlefield. They were used extensively in the First World War, proving almost impervious to the sound of gun fire whilst in flight and less susceptible to the effects of gas than human beings.

Three soldiers carrying the component parts of a short-range wireless station, the British Field Wireless Set (BF Set), May 1917. At the start of the war wireless installations were large and bulky. The rapid development of battery and wireless telegraphy over a few short years saw the introduction of the first man-pack equipment.

The BF Set erected and being tested. This set had an output of 50 watts and was developed from the Stirling Spark Transmitter and the receivers used by the Royal Flying Corps. The aerial was rather conspicuous and liable to attract gun fire.

A *Marconi portable wireless station* used in the First World War. Four horses were required to convey this complete station using special rigid pack saddles. Most wireless stations were mounted in wagons though many types of animal transport were utilized in different parts of the world including mules, elephants and camels.

Linemen laying underground cable in the First World War. From early in 1915 cable was being buried in shallow trenches as a protection against traffic and shrapnel. Later cables were armoured and buried six or more feet deep to prevent damage from direct shelling. The Signal Service subaltern with his cable and the weary infantry working party digging it in by the light of star-shells became a familiar feature in forward areas.

Second Lieutenant (later Lieutenant Colonel) Tom Unwin, mounted centre, with 13th Signal Company Royal Engineers at Cowshot before embarking for France, November 1915. Lieutenant Unwin commanded his Line Section at Ypres, the Somme and Passchendaele. He was twice mentioned in despatches and awarded the Belgian Croix de Guerre. In the Second World War he became a founder member of the Royal Electrical and Mechanical Engineers. Tragically, having survived two world wars, he and three colleagues were murdered by terrorists in Haifa in 1947. His son, Major Peter Unwin, served in the Royal Corps of Signals.

Corporal (later Lieutenant Colonel) C.R.G. Bassett VC of the New Zealand Divisional Signal Company. Corporal Bassett was awarded the Victoria Cross at Gallipoli for his brave action on 7 August 1915. After the New Zealand Infantry Brigade had captured Chunuk Bair Ridge, Corporal Bassett succeeded in laying a telephone line from the old position to the new in broad daylight and under continuous and heavy fire.

The Fullerphone in use in the trenches, 1916. At the beginning of the war civilian telephones met the rapidly increasing need for communications but conversations over tele-phone lines were easy for the enemy to overhear. Captain (later Major-General) A.C. Fuller then invented an instrument, the Fullerphone, which not only provided a telephone circuit but also a telegraph (hand-speed Morse) circuit which almost impossible to inter-cept. A contemporary (unknown) 'poet' wrote, 'And thus the Fullerphone was made. It greatly hurts the Kaiser, because we buzz away all day and he is none the wiser.'

Royal Engineer Signallers using a telescope and Lucas Lamp at the Battle of Arras, April 1917. Early in the war, visual signalling fell into disfavour since the lamps worked by accumulators and were not very portable. In addition, a wide dispersion of beam rendered signalling vulnerable to enemy interception. The new Lucas Lamp, operated with dry cell batteries, was not only lighter but had increased strength, efficiency of component parts and a markedly reduced dispersion of beam.

Indian Signal Service Cable Wagon, Mesopotamia, 1917. A division, which included the 34th Signal Company Sappers and Miners and the Wireless Signal Squadron, was despatched to Mesopotamia in 1914 to protect the Anglo-Persian oil installations from the Turks. The campaign lasted until 1918 when the Turks were finally defeated at Sharquat. Signallers played a vital part in conditions of terrible heat and great hardship.

Mark V Tank with a Semaphore Instrument. Communication between tanks, involving a system of control posts linked by poled route to the cable head, was proving ineffective. After the battle of Cambrai, where tanks were used in large numbers, accelerated development of armoured communication was deemed vital. Wireless telegraphy was tried for inter-tank working and, by 1918, radio telephony from tank to tank and tank to aircraft was being attempted.

Royal Engineer Signal Service members taking part in the Armistice Parade at Bedford, 1919. Throughout the course of the war Signals never rested and were involved in vital and exacting work undertaken bravely, patiently and reliably. The Army appreciated their efforts and wherever the blue and white armband appeared its owners were made welcome. But the cost was great and signallers fell in France and Flanders, Italy and Salonika and the deserts of Iraq and Palestine as well as in East Africa.

'Through' by Francis Martin. The word 'through' has always been used by signallers to confirm that communications have been established between the ends of a link. This depiction of an unnamed lineman lying dead in No-Man's Land after having repaired a broken cable, encapsulates the ideal of the signaller which is to get his message 'through' regardless of the cost or difficulty. As an official dispatch at the end of the war said, 'The Signal Service met the calls made upon it in a manner wholly admirable.'

Two
From 1920 to 1938

The Royal Warrant.
The Signal Service
expanded greatly
during the First
World War and good
communications
became essential to
effective command
and staff work.
Although still part of
the Royal Engineers,
the Service was
virtually a separate
entity and, in
consequence, on 28
June 1920 a Corps of
Signals was formed.
In recognition of the
tremendous
contribution made by
the Signal Service to
the war effort, the
Royal Warrant was
conferred on the
Corps in August of
the same year. The
Warrant was signed
by Winston
Churchill, Secretary
of State for War.

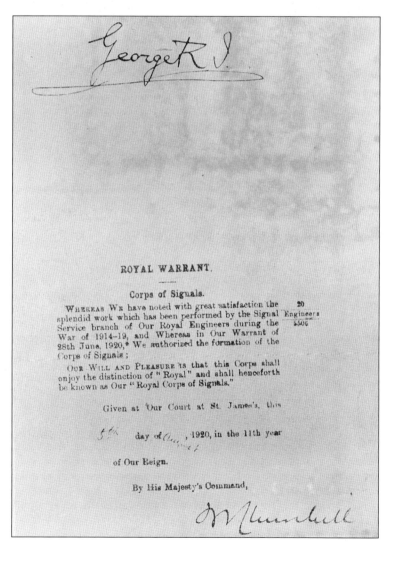

ROYAL WARRANT.

Corps of Signals.

WHEREAS WE have noted with great satisfaction the splendid work which has been performed by the Signal Service branch of Our Royal Engineers during the War of 1914–19, and Whereas in Our Warrant of 28th June, 1920,* We authorized the formation of the Corps of Signals;

OUR WILL AND PLEASURE IS that this Corps shall enjoy the distinction of "Royal" and shall henceforth be known as Our "Royal Corps of Signals."

Given at Our Court at St. James's, this

5th day of Aug, 1920, in the 11th year

of Our Reign.

By His Majesty's Command,

Lieutenant General Sir John Fowler KCB KCMG DSO, first Colonel Commandant of the Royal Corps of Signals. General Fowler was commissioned into the Royal Engineers in 1886 and saw service in a number of campaigns including Chitral and the North West Frontier. During the South African War he was Director Telegraph Service of the Orange Free State and subsequently became first Commander of the Army Signal School in 1913. Throughout the First World War he was Director of Signals to the British Expeditionary Force. His tenure of office as Colonel Commandant of the Corps lasted from 1923 until 1934.

The Mansion, Maresfield Park Camp, Sussex, first Headquarter Mess of the Royal Corps of Signals. Following demobilisation in 1919 all elements of the Royal Engineers Signal Service consolidated at Maresfield Park Camp, forming the Signal Training Centre and School of Signals, under the command of Brigadier-General E.G. Godfrey Fausset CB CMG. The Corps remained in Maresfield until 1925 when it moved to Catterick.

Jimmy Emblem – Boxing Champion, 1921. The new Corps was quick to show its mettle in the world of sport, winning Army Championships in athletics, boxing and cross-country running. Jimmy was a successful middleweight boxing champion and, though the origin of the affectionate term 'Jimmy' for the Corps badge is not known, it seems possible that he was the inspiration. Interestingly too, the sporting colours, a red Mercury on a white background, awarded to members of the Royal Engineer Signal Service and later the Royal Corps of Signals, were called 'Jimmies'.

Signalman Ballard and Lance Corporal Morphew competing in the First Corps Boxing Championships at Maresfield Park, July 1921. One of the officials was Lieutenant Harry Spencer MC, a boxing champion who widely promoted boxing and ensured that the sport remained amateur in the Services.

The Corps Band, 1923. In 1921 a few ex-members of the Royal Engineers Depot Band formed the nucleus of a Corps Band at Maresfield Park. The Band did not receive official recognition until 1938 and until then all members provided their services voluntarily whilst also undertaking their roles as signallers. The Officers paid for the services of the bandmaster.

The Royal Signals Choir. The Choir were winners of the Northern England Championships in the early 1920s and the Choirmaster, Mr Randolph Ricketts, seated in the centre of the front row, was Corps Bandmaster from 1926 to 1938. Mr Ricketts was a distinguished musician, talented at both composition and arrangement. Under the pseudonym Leo Stanley, he published numerous marches and other well-known military music including 'HRH The Princess Royal' which was adopted as the Corps Slow March in 1952. His brother, F.J. Ricketts was Director of Music of the Royal Marines and composer of the famous march 'Colonel Bogie'.

The Bedale Hunt outside the Royal Signals' Officers Mess, Catterick, 1926. After considerable debate about location for a permanent home for the Training Centre and Headquarters Mess Royal Signals, Catterick was selected. The Army's intention was to construct an 'Aldershot of the North' to accommodate the Army of the Rhine on its return to the United Kingdom. Catterick provided close contact with units of other arms for both training and sport and so was an ideal choice.

Type 'A' Soldiers' Married Quarters, Catterick. In a major rebuilding programme undertaken at Catterick Camp in 1924 barrack blocks were converted to married quarters. The building contractor was John Laing & Son and the quarters shown in the photograph were in occupation until the late 1950s.

Captain Skinner at the heliograph station on the roof of GHQ Constantinople, 1921. In the inter-war years signallers contributed to occupation forces, garrisons and expeditions throughout the world. By coincidence, General Sir Charles Harrington, Commander in Chief British Army in Constantinople in 1921, was a staunch supporter of the Corps and had been instrumental in its formation.

The Cable Ship Levant *off Chenak, Turkey, 1923.* In 1922 a combined British naval and military force went to the Dardanelles to prevent Kemal Attaturk from seizing the straits connecting the Aegean with the Sea of Marmora. 2nd Divisional Signals were based near Chenak and the *Levant* provided cables for communication, across the straits to the heavy artillery in Gallipoli and to GHQ in Constantinople. Launched in 1906, the *Levant* also took part in the First World War Dardanelles campaign.

Training in the use of telescope and Lucas Lamp, 1920s. Equipment saw little change in the early years and the signalling lamp remained in service until well after the Second World War. The battery-operated signalling lamp was readable with the naked eye to a distance of two miles in bright sunlight and up to six miles at night. When viewed through a telescope, the day and night ranges of the lamp were extended to about four and twelve miles respectively.

A Detachment of 'F' Company Training Battalion, Royal Signals at Carville Power Station in the General Strike of 1926. The Depression of the early 1920s had resulted in high unemployment and there was bitter conflict in the coal industry where wage cuts were imposed. In April 1926 the executives of 141 Trade Unions called a national strike in support of the miners. Power Station workers were among the first to 'down tools' and the Detachment of 'F' Company was one of many military units drafted in to help keep vital power supplies going.

Winners of the Non Commissioned Officer's Show Jumping Championships at Olympia, 1932. From left to right: Corporal Bull, Company Sergeant Major Young, Corporal Meldrum and Sergeant Bennett. Equestrian events were not just a matter of sport. The standard of horsemanship required of Royal Signals personnel was high. Cable-laying in particular demanded the control of a team of six horses pulling a wagon at speed co-ordinated with the efforts of a number of other mounted soldiers.

Royal Signals (Northern Command, India) Polo Team. From left to right: Lieutenant L.D.M. Patterson, Lieutenant G.S. Knox, Captain (later Major-General) C.M.F. White and Lieutenant (later Major-General) A.M.W. Whistler. The team beat fifteen entries to win the Abbottabad Spring Tournament of 1934. In the same Command, the 1st Cavalry Brigade Signal Troop swept the board in the Other Ranks Handy Hunters Competition and Hunter Trials.

Lieutenant Henry Crawford on 'Hot Pot' winning the Royal West Show, 1932. Lieutenant Crawford, an accomplished horseman was a founder member of the Corps Display Team.

The Royal Signals Display Team. The Team, formed in 1927 provided an excellent opportunity for its members to hone the very necessary skills of teamwork, horsemanship and motorbike riding. Breathtaking tricks, involving horses and bikes moving at speed provided exciting entertainment and the team were much in demand appearing in shows and regularly at the Royal Tournament. The motorcycles were provided by Triumph Engineering Company and to this day the team continue to use British machines.

King George V, Queen Mary and The Princess Royal at Mons Barracks, April 1932. The Royal visit to Mons Barracks, which was specially built for the Royal Corps of Signals in 1926, marked the coming of age of the Corps. Among many displays and demonstrations mounted for the Royal visitors was the Baby Austin car, in the centre of the photograph, which was fitted with wireless telephone.

John William Agar. In 1933 HM The King relayed his personal condolences to the parents of Lieutenant John Agar following his tragic death. Lieutenant Agar drowned in 1933, while rescuing two Signalmen from his section who got into difficulties in the water off Studland, near Swanage. There is a memorial to Lieutenant Agar in the Chapel at the Royal Military Academy Sandhurst and a prize, commemorating his sacrifice and service to his soldiers, is awarded to the best cadet in each intake entering Royal Signals.

W.M. (Joe) Cotterell, 1921.
William 'Joe' Cotterell was one
of the most outstanding athletes
in the Army. During the 1920s
he was an international
champion at both cross-country
running and long distance track
events and he represented
Britain at the 1924 Olympic
Games in Paris.

Lieutenant (later Brigadier) C.H. Stoneley hands over the baton to Lieutenant Rampling in the 4x440 yards relay race to win a Bronze Medal at the British Empire Games, 1934. Lieutenant Stoneley also represented Great Britain in the 1932 Olympic Games in which he won a Silver Medal as a member of the 4x440 yards relay team.

Lieutenant E.C. Thompson and Lieutenant (later Brigadier CBE DSO ACE FRGS) Smijth-Windham, 1933 Everest Expedition. Expedition organisers of the 1930s recognised the value of the ever-increasing improvement in communications and Royal Signals personnel were much in demand by adventurers and explorers as wireless operators. Lieutenants E.C. Thompson and W.R. Smijth-Windham, Sergeant Watt and Corporal Frawley were lent by the Government of India to the Everest Expedition of 1933. Thompson and Smijth-Windham accompanied the expedition to 21,000ft and 22,800ft respectively and broke the world record for working wireless stations at altitude.

Lieutenant Ian F. Meiklejohn, Wireless Officer to the British Grahamland Expedition in Antarctica. A group, under the leadership of Mr J.R. Rymill (a member of the Watkins Arctic Air Route Expedition), left England in the autumn of 1934 for a three-year expedition to Grahamland in Antarctica. Lieutenant I.F. Meiklejohn was in charge of wireless communications and was subsequently awarded the Polar Medal.

Major (later Brigadier) R.A. Bagnold and Lieutenant (later Brigadier CBE) D.W.R. Burridge with a fellow explorer in the Western Desert, 1929. Major Bagnold, son of Colonel A.H. Bagnold who served in 'C' Troop, undertook a number of expeditions and explorations in the 1920s and 1930s in the deserts of Africa. He was the author of the definitive work on the movement of desert sands, providing vital information still in use by desert travellers today. Among many of his inventions were the Sun Compass and the sand channel, a device to aid movement of vehicles through sand dunes. Major Bagnold was to put his extensive knowledge of the desert to good use in the Second World War.

Captain Tozer with his detachment of the North China Signal Section outside the British Military HQ, Tientsin in the early 1930s. After its formation in 1920 Royal Signals ran and maintained a network of overseas stations known as the Army Chain. The function of this organisation was intelligence gathering via the interception and monitoring of local communications. The task was necessary at a time when the Army was engaged on active service in many parts of the Empire. The China group of stations was established in Tientsin, Peking and Hong Kong in 1932.

Part of the city of Quetta, India, after the Earthquake of 1935. Three quarters of the city was devastated by the earthquake, communications were destroyed and thousands of people were killed. Royal Signals and their Indian Signal Corps comrades were part of the Garrison of Quetta and, fortunately, the Royal Signals barracks was undamaged. From here a massive rescue operation was launched. Communications with the outside world were quickly established and a hugely successful human relief operation was mounted by Corps personnel.

The Royal Signals Temporary Telegraph Office set up in Quetta to deal with the relief operation after the earthquake. The Royal Signals' contribution to the relief effort was vital and was acknowledged by the Commander in Chief: 'All soldiers responded to the call splendidly but it was the Signals who enabled the work to be co-ordinated and effective. Please tell them how much I admire their work.'

Drive Past for King's Birthday, Canterbury, 1935. Back home routine peacetime soldiering continued and in Canterbury 4th Division Signals marked the occasion of the birthday of King George V with a parade. Lieutenant Colonel Henderson, mounted on 'Gunner', takes the salute.

The Princess Royal at Catterick on 8 October 1936 with Brigadier Heyman, Colonel Chevenix Trench, Brigadier Clementi Smith and Major G. Taylor. In 1935 HM The King appointed HRH The Princess Mary, The Princess Royal, to be Colonel in Chief of the Royal Corps of Signals and her visit to Catterick in October of the following year was her first to the Corps.

The No.1 Wireless Set mounted in a car, 1936. In parallel with support to the Empire and consolidation at home, concepts and techniques were changing. In post-war expansion of Army wireless equipment, a series of sets was developed, numbered from 1 to 6. Numbers 1, 2 and 3 were designed to work on the move and could be mounted in a vehicle or carried by pack animal. The sets were robust but suffered from inadequate power and range in relation to weight.

The No.1 Wireless Set mounted on a horse in Waziristan on the North West Frontier c. 1937. In the years between the wars the main overseas station of the Corps was India. Waziristan was a barren and inhospitable area where disputes between tribesmen and incursions by the Afghans contributed to a volatile climate. During the Waziristan Operations of 1936-1937 the first two Corps DSOs were won by Lieutenant Colonel C.H.H. Vulliamy and Lieutenant Colonel W.R.C. Penny, both of whom later became Major Generals.

56th (London) Divisional Signals demonstrated early mechanisation for cable laying using a half-tracked motor vehicle. After the First World War mechanisation was introduced slowly and some units were a mixture of motor and horse drawn vehicles, making the handling of signal sections extremely difficult.

56th (London) Divisional Signals with horse-drawn cable wagon take part in the ceremonial of the Lord Mayor's Show in London, 1930. Horse-drawn units continued to have a greater appeal for ceremonial duties. The descendants of this unit, 56th Signal Squadron, part of 31st (City of London) Signal Regiment, still today take part in City of London ceremonial.

The last mounted parade of 'B' Cable Section, 2nd Divisional Signals, Aldershot, 1937. As the Second World War approached mechanisation finally arrived and the horse-drawn cable wagon, in service for over thirty years, was at last consigned to history.

The mechanical cable layer, 1938. The successor to the horse-drawn vehicle was demonstrated in Aldershot in 1938. The mechanical layer was capable of throwing out cable several yards to the side of its track at speeds of up to 20mph. Cable was projected high into the air to fall on top of hedges and into low branches of trees along side roads and could be adjusted to throw cable into a ditch.

Three
From 1939 to 1945

Headquarters 32nd Army Tank Brigade, Tobruk Corridor (Tiger), November 1941. On the eve of the Second World War the Army was not as well prepared for war as in August 1914. The new Corps, however, though short of qualified men and equipment, was well trained and confident. Its strength was 2,000 Officers and 35,000 other ranks including the Territorial Army and Reservists. By VE Day it had quadrupled in size and constituted about five per cent of the Army. This expansion was necessitated by the increase in communications, particularly in lines of communication, a commitment not allowed for in peace. Air power and the mobility produced by mechanisation also called for extra communications.

Linemen of the British Expeditionary Force in Bienville, France 1939. The British Expeditionary Force was despatched to France immediately after the declaration of war in 1939. During the 'phoney' war considerable use was made of civil lines but forward of Corps Headquarters multi air-line was considered vulnerable to bombing. A system using field cable on air-line poles with a big sag to absorb the concussion of explosions proved successful. Wireless was little used and the communications plan was similar to that developed on the Western Front in 1916-1917.

Miss M.A. Carter and her ATS Telephonists, France, 1939. The women's Auxiliary Territorial Service had a signal section very early in the war. The last British personnel to leave Paris, within an hour of the German encirclement of the City, were ATS manning the Trunk Exchange. By 1942 women had taken over the major part of the Signal Office and Command system in the United Kingdom and proved very suitable for certain operating and Signal Office trades. In 1945 the number of women employed on signal duties was one-tenth of the Corps.

Lieutenant Colonel S.A.W. Philcox TD and Officers of No.2 Company, 2nd Corps Signals at Ostricourt, October 1939. The 'phoney' war ended on 10 May 1940 with the German Blitzkrieg which cut Allied Forces in two and reached the channel in ten days. The bulk of the British Expeditionary Force escaped from Dunkirk, ably assisted by the existence of a cable link from La Panne to the United Kingdom, established on the initiative of a junior Signals Officer. The link remained in operation until 1 July when, just hours before withdrawal of the rearguard, the operators were ordered to destroy the teleprinter.

The Colonel in Chief visits 3rd Divisional Signals at Blandford in November 1940. Following Dunkirk the British Army regrouped to face the prospect of invasion. The 3rd Division, previously commanded by General Montgomery, concentrated in the South West as part of 5th Corps and the Divisional Signals moved to Blandford Forum in November 1940. Many well-known landmarks of Blandford were used to house the Regiment. The Corn Exchange became a Mess and function room, the Quartermaster's Stores occupied a shop opposite and the rear of the Crown Hotel provided a vehicle park.

Signallers at work in an armoured wireless car, Egypt. The forces stationed in Egypt had been training for a war in the western desert for several years. The open spaces of the desert proved ideal for wireless and, although the only available sets had inadequate range, Regiments of the Armoured Brigade, Commanders and Staffs relied extensively on wireless communication.

Signalman A.R. Johnson, a Despatch Rider of the Express Letter Service, Egypt, 1941. Italian forces commenced cautious operations in North Africa in 1940 but in a series of brilliant exploits were rebuffed and defeated by the 7th Armoured Division and the 4th Indian Division. As the war progressed development in communication techniques advanced swiftly. However, the Despatch Rider Service, which had proved so invaluable in the First World War, continued to be a necessary element of field communications.

Divisional Headquarters Command Vehicle, The Desert, 1941. Effective command and control in the desert was not easy in an environment of fast moving units over a wide battlefield area with fixed supply systems in the rear. Mobile wireless, therefore, became a primary means of communication forward of Division.

Crew of Armoured Command Vehicle 2nd Headquarters 7th Armoured Division, 1942. The widespread use of telephony had its difficulties and drawbacks. The range of sets available was not adequate and battery charging was a constant problem. Training and confidence between Signals and Staff had, therefore, to be of a high standard if communications were to work efficiently in the stress of battle.

Radio Operators at Sollum-Halfaya, July 1942. With the arrival of the German Afrika Korps under Rommel in March 1941, the desert war became a 'whirling armoured dog-fight' in which fortunes ebbed and flowed. By July 1942, following a series of bitter battles, such as Halfaya (Hell Fire), the 8th Army was on the defensive at El Alamein, only sixty miles short of Alexandria.

The Long Range Desert Group. At the suggestion of Major (later Brigadier) Ralph Bagnold, Royal Signals, the desert explorer of the 1930s, the Long Range Desert Group (LRDG) was formed. The task of the unit was to penetrate far behind enemy lines for reconnaissance and intelligence gathering. In mid-November 1941 Lieutenant Colonel David Stirling and his newly formed Special Air Service parachuted into Gazala on their first mission. The exploit was not a success and subsequently many SAS operations in the desert were mounted from LRDG vehicles. After service in North Africa, LRDG re-equipped for operations in Greece, Italy and Yugoslavia. Sadly, after five very effective years the unit was disbanded in 1945.

Linemen in the Western Desert. At 2140 hours on the night of 23 October 1942 the 8th Army launched its offensive. On 2 November armoured forces broke through the defence line south of the main German strength. The communications plan for this battle included much line, particularly for the artillery. A network of field cables was also laid by cable plough for the Armoured Divisions. The linemen suffered casualties from booby traps as many of the poles and verges of the roads were mined.

British Armoured Command Vehicle (ACV), used by Rommel in the Western Desert. The ACV was developed by Royal Signals as a means of ensuring effective command of mobile armoured units. Commanders, operators and key staff were able to travel and work together in the heavily armoured vehicles. In April 1941 the Germans captured three ACVs and Rommel was so impressed with the concept that he allocated two to members of his staff and retained a third for his own use throughout the North Africa campaign.

Basic Military Training. The rapid expansion of the Corps, the influx of new technology and the ferocity of modern warfare demanded a revitalisation of training. Signallers were required to be tough and robust as well as technically able.

Teleprinter Training. Teleprinters entered military service in 1933. The Defence Telecommunications Network using teleprinters was established in 1939 and was fundamental to the air defence of the country during the Battle of Britain. Co-operation with American forces saw teleprinter operations extended down to Divisional level.

Line Training using models. New methods were introduced into training to help convert mobilised civilians into useful tradesmen as rapidly as possible. Amongst the techniques used was the extensive use of high quality models or 'simulations' as they would be called today.

Training in Signal Office Clerk duties. Lessons from operations were learned quickly and turned into effective training. Soldiers were taught the techniques that they would find in use in the operational theatres to enable them to take their place as useful members of the team immediately on arrival.

Pigeons being used by Airborne Forces, 1942. Royal Signals took over responsibility for the Carrier Pigeon Service in 1920 and Loftsman became a trade within the Corps. 157 pigeon lofts were established in the Second World War, both in the United Kingdom and overseas. Pigeons were dropped by parachute to resistance groups enabling them to send messages to England thus eliminating the necessity for radio transmissions which could be easily intercepted. Airborne Forces used pigeons on D-Day and at Arnhem. The trade of Loftsman ceased in 1946.

Captain McConnell Wood testing a pack set for communication back to base, with the Camel Brigade, Jordan, 1943.

On the beach, the Sicily Landings, 1943. Following the success of the 8th Army and the Allied Operation Torch in securing North Africa, the first invasion of the European mainland was undertaken in Sicily. One of the main problems encountered in the assault was the danger of damage to signal equipment by sea water; this led to the development of very thorough waterproofing methods.

Line laying in action in the Italian Campaign. The Allied advance in Italy was checked at the line of the rivers Sangro and Garigliano. A very large number of circuits was required for the land and air forces and operations were conducted over mountainous country in difficult weather conditions.

Major General W.R.C. Penney CB CBE DSO MC (late R Signals), at Anzio, 1943. By the end of 1943 it became clear that the Germans intended to put up fierce resistance to the Allied advance. Allied strength was limited, landing craft had been withdrawn for the invasion of Normandy and thus the scope for turning the enemy's flank was restricted. However, the 1st Armoured Division, commanded by Major General Penney was a key element in the amphibious landing at Anzio. Major General Penney was severely wounded in the action. Lieutenant Colonel Stoneley commanded the Divisional Signals during the battle and subsequent actions.

Action at the Anzio bridgehead. Following the Anzio assault a succession of frontal attacks had to be made over mountainous country and every advance was bitterly contested. The basis of the communications plan continued to be the line system.

Signalman Bartholomew and colleagues on his invention, the motorcycle cable layer. Innovation and initiative were vital to overcome the difficulties of field cable laying and maintenance in such difficult terrain. It is estimated that Royal Signals laid some 3 million miles of line and cable during the Second World War.

Checking signal lines near a Bailey Bridge over the Osento. Main signal line arteries ran either side of the central Italian mountains with lateral routes across them. These overhead routes were built and maintained in the face of great difficulties, particularly in winter. Efficient communications were thus provided even when complete Corps or Armies were transferred from one side of the 'front' to the other, which happened twice.

Sergeant A. Banks and Lance Corporal E. Herd operate a switchboard with 5th US Army, Italy, 1944.
Signal detachments were attached to the 5th US Army to maintain liaison. Signal communications during the Italian campaign reached a high pitch of efficiency and a balance of methods probably not attained in any other theatre. There was a pooling of communication resources and signal units of different nationalities developed a remarkable ability to work together without dislocation.

Lance Corporal C Jarman operates main Corps switchboard on a 3-ton lorry with 5th US Army.

A *Dispatch Rider hands over his message, Italy, 1944.* The Italian campaign required harder fighting over a longer continuous period than in any other theatre and greatly influenced the development of signal methods. New technology, such as radio relay to supplement line, and increased use of VHF had a considerable effect. But, as in so many other battles, Dispatch Riders displayed great courage and determination in backing up these innovations.

The Wireless Set Type 3, Mark 2 ('Suitcase Set'). In the shadows behind more conventional operations, the Special Operations Executive encouraged resistance to the occupiers of conquered territory in Europe and the Far East. They relied heavily on Royal Signals and could not have functioned without the aid of the Corps. Wireless operators used a 'suitcase' radio, designed by Lieutenant (later Major) J.I. Brown, Royal Signals. Ahead of the D-Day landings thirteen small teams, each consisting of an American and French soldier with a British radio operator with his suitcase set, were parachuted into France to help co-ordinate the efforts of the Resistance. They were the 'Jedburgh' teams and the suitcase radio is, therefore, sometimes referred to as the 'Jedburgh set'.

Sergeant Phillips of the Special Operations Executive. Sergeant Phillips, accompanied by Signalman Stewart, volunteered to work behind German lines in Italy. On one occasion they were hiding in the top part of a house whilst a German patrol occupied the ground floor. During the night Sergeant Phillips crept down among the sleeping enemy and connected his low batteries to their charger.

Phantom, operating the R107 Receiver. The Corps provided other unconventional support including Phantom and the J Service. Phantom was the GHQ Liaison Regiment consisting of Royal Signals personnel and other Arms, mainly cavalry, who were all trained in signals techniques. Phantom monitored transmissions and passed information, on locations of our own forward troops, directly back to GHQ. The J Service, created by Major Mainwaring in 1941, monitored enemy transmissions and sent the gleanings to GHQ. Phantom and the J Service merged in December 1944 and played an important part in operations from D-Day to the end of the war.

Signalman Smith GC. Signalman Kenneth Smith, part of a Long Range Desert Group patrol based on Ist, an island off Yugoslavia, was awarded a posthumous George Cross for his valour in an incident in January 1945. One night fascist partisans dropped a large time bomb into the house in which he was billeted. Without a thought for his safety Signalman Smith quickly removed his radio equipment and then, remembering the family asleep in the building, picked up the bomb and rushed for a nearby open space. The bomb exploded and he was killed.

Below: '*Smith GC*'. From a painting by Peter Archer.

With the Chindits in Burma. In December 1941 Japan entered the war and by February 1942 had overrun Malaya, Singapore and Hong Kong. The Japanese then turned on Burma and the Commonwealth forces retreated to the Indian frontier. The Chindits mounted major, deep penetration raids to harry the enemy. Wireless was vital and was operated in tough conditions. Difficulties such as high humidity were overcome by better packing and sealing but it was dedication and experience of signallers that made wireless work efficiently and reliably.

Supplies being dropped to the Chindits by parachute. Air supply was developed on a far greater scale than in any other theatre and special Signal units were organised to provide the necessary communications. Air despatch messages became very important and homing sets were used to guide aircraft to improvised landing strips and dropping zones.

Signalling within range of the Japanese in Burma. The battles of Imphal and Kohima on the Indian border marked the turning point of operations in Burma. Signallers were in the thick of the fighting and frequently took part in counter-attacks as well as maintaining communications.

Field cable laying, Imphal, Kohima and Burma. Line communications were particularly important in defence and in the early stages of the campaign to free Burma. Military routes were extensions of those of the Indian Posts and Telegraph system. Corridors were cut through the jungle and, further forward, insulated cables were slung from trees.

Horsa Glider being towed by a Halifax bomber, over Blandford Camp, 5 June 1944. Ahead of the amphibious landings for D-Day a glider-borne force of 6th Airborne Division took off from Tarrant Rushton bound for the bridges over the River Orne and Caen Canal in Normandy. Capture of these crossing points was vital to protect the left flank of the seaborne invasion. In extremely difficult conditions and pitch darkness, Sergeant Roy Howard, Royal Signals, piloted the only one of three gliders destined for the Orne bridge to reach its target. On landing he joined the assault party and, for his brilliant efforts, was awarded the Distinguished Flying Medal.

Commando Signallers on the Normandy beaches – D-Day. On 6 June 1944 Operation Overlord was launched. Three Airborne Divisions landed in Normandy during the night and at dawn the landing craft approached the beaches. Signal units were among the first ashore. Assault communications were based on wireless and achieved a remarkable degree of success. Reserve communication resources held in the beach Signal troops were hardly needed.

Corporal Waters MM. Corporal Waters in the uniform of the King's Own Yorkshire Light Infantry, the crossed flags on his arm indicate that he was a Regimental signaller. After seeing action in Burma, India and China he attained the rank of Sergeant but took a drop in rank to Corporal to join Airborne Signals for D-Day. Corporal Waters earned the Military Medal on D-Day when he rescued three wounded comrades and then, under continued intense enemy fire, laid and maintained a line across the Caen Canal bridge to 7th Parachute Battalion. He was invalided out of the Army in May 1945 after a training accident but then died tragically in 1955 after being knocked down by a car.

Below: *Go to It*. From a painting by Peter Archer depicting Corporal Water's Action on the Caen Canal Bridge, Benouville, 6 June 1944.

Laying cable under fire. For the rest of June and early July 1944 Allied Armies were contained in a small area. Communications functioned well though there were problems due to extreme congestion on the roads and continued enemy interference. After heavy fighting, the battle for Normandy was won in late August.

Field linemen construct airline during the Allied advance. The rate of advance from Normandy to the east was extremely rapid and the building of land line communications could not keep up with the progress of the armies.

The No.10 Set. Mobile radio link equipment, such as the No.10 Set proved its worth during the advance, providing the only communications between Main and Tactical Army Group Headquarters on many occasions. This British radio was the first multi-channel, ultra high frequency radio relay equipment in the world. It enabled the carriage of up to eight simultaneous telephone conversations and its signals were concentrated in a narrow beam which increased range and security. By 1945 a chain of No.10 Set relay stations stretched from Luneburg in Germany to Brussels.

'*Golden Arrow*'. Despite the speed of advance Army Group Headquarters had to maintain communications with the War Office. The Golden Arrow radio station had been tried and tested in India and Italy. With a power of at least 3kW this mobile transmitter was comparable to a medium powered broadcast station. It could be erected and in action, sending high speed morse, within three hours of arrival. The station consisted of five vehicles and two trailers that closely resembled railway carriages, giving the radio station its name. There was a crew of one officer and twenty-two signallers, each selected for outstanding ability demonstrated during preliminary training.

Lance Corporal R.W. Bennett MM receiving congratulations from General (later Field Marshall Viscount) Montgomery of Alamein after receiving a bar to his Military Medal. Lance Corporal Bennett won a Military Medal for conspicuous gallantry in 1943 when a wireless operator and driver to 30th Corps Liaison Staff in the desert. The Bar to his Decoration was won on D-Day. Corporal Bennett was commanding a large and unwieldy communications vehicle on a beach constantly swept by shell and mortar fire. In the absence of the Tactical HQ, which had been unable to land, he provided the sole means of communication for 30th Corps to the mainland.

An Enigma Machine. The greatest secret of the Second World War was 'Ultra', the code name for the decryption of German secret wireless traffic encoded by the ingenious Enigma machine. This decryption process depended upon successful radio interception by operators in the Royal Signals 'Y Service', an organisation so secret its existence was not even revealed to Senior Commanders. 'Y' Service units served in all theatres of operation and their contribution to the tactical, operational and strategic success in the Second World War cannot be overstated.

Lieutenant Colonel Jimmy Yule. Lieutenant Colonel Yule was captured in May 1940 and, after many escape attempts, was moved to the notorious Colditz Castle. As a Royal Signals Officer Jimmy was the natural choice to control a secret radio station set up in Colditz by French Officers who had been transferred to another prison. He monitored Allied and enemy broadcasts and kept his fellow prisoners informed on progress of the war. The nature of this morale-boosting task convinced him he should not undertake further escape attempts. He also raised spirits by organising musical theatricals, the noise of which were sometimes deliberately used to drown out the sound of escape preparations.

The secret radio station in Colditz Castle. The wireless room, only rediscovered in 1993, was located in a tiny space in the castle roof. Its site was known to only six prisoners who worked the station in two teams of three: an operator, a listener and a look-out. The radio was powered from the castle supply and the hide was furnished with maps to make the news from Allied and German broadcasts more intelligible. In other prison camps, including those in the Far East, Royal Signals personnel used their skills to build radio sets from improvised components which were instrumental in maintaining the morale of Allied prisoners.

Major General Phillips, Major General Vulliamy and Colonel French with the Bronze Plaque presented to Royal Signals by the US Signal Corps, July 1946. At the end of the Second World War the US Signal Corps and the Royal Corps of Signals exchanged tokens as a mark of mutual admiration and appreciation of the special and close co-operation which had existed between them. This relationship resulted in the delivery of a high standard of communications in many theatres of operations. Perhaps the main lesson for the Corps of the Second World War was the vital importance of individual responsibility and teamwork between signallers within units and between signal units of many different nations. Only a common allegiance and unified control made it possible to link them together in providing a single communications' system. By the end of the war 4,631 signallers had lost their lives in the Service of their country but the principles and traditions of Royal Signals were finally and firmly established.

Four
From 1946 to 1961

King Hussein of Jordan with Major (later Major-General OBE) D.R. Horsfield in 1952. Major David Horsfield, Royal Signals, Commander of Inkerman Company at the Royal Military Academy Sandhurst, was selected from a distinguished body of twelve Company Commanders to have charge of this prestigious overseas Officer Cadet. A fitting responsibility for a member of a Corps that had more than satisfied its commanders in two great wars.

Bombing of the King David Hotel, 1946. At the end of the war the Corps faced contraction to its peacetime establishment as well as accommodating the influx of National Servicemen. The bleak economic outlook for Britain precluded development or investment in new equipment but operational commitments still had to be met, the first of these in Palestine where conflict raged between Jews and Arabs. The Kind David Hotel which housed the Operations Room of HQ Palestine and Transjordan was bombed by terrorists on 22 July 1946 causing a number of casualties. Royal Signals personnel, aided by Arab and Jewish Post Office workers, who worked extremely well together, quickly re-established communications.

SQMS F. Bolton, BEM servicing an RAF 20 Line Keyboard during the Berlin Airlift 1948. In June 1948 Russia, occupying one sector of Berlin, cut off all communication from the west by road and rail through their zone. The citizens were thus starved of supplies and the Western powers spent the next eleven months flying in food, coal and other essentials night and day from eight airfields to Gatow in Berlin. Communications were vital and Royal Signals played a major part in the operation.

Transmitter and Receiver Room of the War Office Signal Regiment. The Regiment was raised at the outset of the Second World War to handle all War Office military signal traffic, other than telephone, and to man the Army Chain wireless stations. On 2 June 1953 the Regiment provided twelve Dispatch Riders to rush television film of the HM The Queen's Coronation to BBC studios for processing prior to its being flown by air to Canada for screening to audiences the very same day.

16th Airborne Division Signals (Middlesex Yeomanry) TA, Coronation Duties, 1953. Many units of Royal Signals contributed to the smooth running of the Coronation ceremonial. Communications controlled the movement of troops and the processions throughout the day. Three hundred men of the Corps marched in the Procession from Buckingham Palace and the Chief Signal Officer, London District, gave a signal from Westminster Abbey for the guns at the Tower to be fired at the exact moment of the crowning.

Reading of Presidential Citation to Brigadier Coad, Commander 27th Brigade and the Brigade Signal Squadron, Korea, 1952. On 25 June 1950 Communist North Korea invaded the non-communist and weaker territory of the South. The United Nations responded by deploying a force of American troops. The British 27th Brigade with other Commonwealth units arrived in August to fight and face both the North Koreans and the Chinese. Hostilities finally ended in July 1953.

29th Independent Infantry Brigade Signal Squadron, Korea 1951. The Squadron included battalion and regimental Rear Link Detachments one of which was attached to the 1st Battalion, the Gloucestershire Regiment. This photograph was taken shortly after the Battle of the Imjin River in which most of this Battalion, hopelessly outnumbered by Chinese forces, were either killed or captured. The members of the Rear Link Detachment, Royal Signals were Lance Corporal Sid Ward, Signalman John Cairns, Signalman (later Major) Henry Jennings and Driver Arthur Miles all of whom were taken prisoner.

The Colonel in Chief accompanied by Lieutenant Colonel C.T. Honeybourne and Major J.E.V. Rice, 7th Armoured Division Signal Regiment in Germany, May 1955. By 1950 the British Army of the Rhine (BAOR), part of the Allied occupation force in Germany, had been reduced to two Divisions, 7th Armoured Division and 2nd Infantry Division. However, as the Cold War developed BAOR was reinforced by the reformed 6th and 11th Armoured Divisions and in 1951 1st British Corps was re-established. Royal Signals, like others, spent much time over the next thirty years training to meet the perceived threat from the Soviet Union.

HMS Johnson, *Suez 1956.* Britain and France mounted a successful military operation to re-open the vital Suez Canal route to international shipping after it was seized and closed by Egypt in 1956. An airborne force, with a Royal Signals element was first into action. 23rd Corps Signal Regiment deployed in November 1957 and commandeered a launch which they named HMS *Johnson*, after their Commanding Officer Lieutenant Colonel (later Colonel) Peter Johnson. HMS *Johnson* operated as a Boat Dispatch Service, perhaps the first and last of its kind ever in the Corps.

Special Air Service personnel awaiting helicopters at 'Paddy's Ladan', Malaya 1955. Two of the party are Royal Signals soldiers. Communications have been a vital part of all SAS operations undertaken since the Second World War. Note the Iban tracker in the rear of the picture who was a member of the Sarawak Rangers.

Gurkha Royal Signals in Malaya. Gurkha soldiers first served as signallers with the Indian Signal Corps in 1917 and subsequently in many theatres of war. On Indian Independence, Gurkha Signal units were raised to provide communications to the newly formed Gurkha Infantry Division of the British Army. In September 1954 the Royal Signals cap badge was replaced with a new badge incorporating the crossed kukris, symbolic of the martial traditions of Nepal. HM The Queen granted her Royal Title in 1977 and the Regiment became the Queen's Gurkha Signals.

A Lance Corporal and Driver, Cyprus, 1958. In 1955 a terrorist group called EOKA launched a campaign of sabotage in Cyprus in support of its aim for union with Greece. A state of emergency, which was to last four years, was declared. During this and in later periods of unrest, Royal Signals played an important part. One task involved the manning of a Radio Relay station on top of Mount Olympus (6,400ft) in the Troodos mountain range, a cold, lonely and exposed outpost vulnerable to terrorist attacks. The station provided essential communications not only to troops around the island but also for the Main and Brigade Command Nets, the Royal Air Force Police, coastal radar sites and minesweepers on anti-smuggling patrols.

Captain (later Major-General and Admiral of the Corps Yacht Club) John Alexander aboard Ganga Devi. There is a long tradition of sailing in the Corps which has been encouraged by the Corps Committee as a means of developing character and self-reliance. John Alexander, then a member of 246 Gurkha Signal Squadron, and a crew of two sailed *Ganga Devi*, a twenty-two-foot sloop, from Hong Kong to England in 1960.

30th Signal Regiment, Arrival Parade in Blandford, 25 May 1960. 30th Signal Regiment, which had endured a turbulent few years moving from Colchester and then to Middle Wallop, was the first operational Signal unit to serve in Blandford Camp. Early in the decade, the Ministry of Defence also decided to relocate the School of Signals from Catterick to Blandford, a site selected for its proximity to the Signals Research and Development Establishment at Christchurch and to other Arms Schools.

Corporal Len Manning (rear left) and colleagues of the AER, Blandford Camp 1961. Headquarters Army Emergency Reserve (AER) moved from Chester to Blandford in 1961. The unit was commanded by a Colonel and staffed by a small cadre of regular and National Service soldiers. A specialist reserve organisation recruited nationally, its members were only required to carry out annual training. The Headquarters of its successor, 81 Signal Squadron (V), is now based in Corsham, Wiltshire. 1960 saw the last call-up of National Servicemen, the end of an era that had lasted since the close of the Second World War. Thereafter the Corps would once again be made up exclusively of volunteers.

Five
From 1962 to 1974

'Moving In', a painting by Ken Howard depicting elements of 22nd Signal Regiment on exercise with BRUIN communications equipment in Germany. The potential nuclear battlefield presented 1950s and '60s communicators with significant challenges. The old cable and line method was inadequate, vulnerable and inflexible. Also, improved weapon systems and the emergence of 'behind the lines' invading forces rendered previously secure headquarters, which carried the bulk of signals traffic, susceptible to attack. Any new communications system had to address these concerns and provide security, robustness, reliability and interoperability with our NATO Allies. Many years of research were needed to reach a solution but, in the interim, a highly successful system named BRUIN was introduced.

'Purdyfoot' Mascot of The Pathfinders Youth Club with soldiers of 216 Signal Squadron, 1964. After the end of National Service the Army began a recruiting drive in an effort to attract high quality volunteers to the Armed Forces. To this end, the Corps adopted The Pathfinders, a youth club in Slough. The Club promoted fitness and good citizenship among its members so making them excellent potential recruits. It was the first time such a link had been forged and, as a sign of gratitude, the Club presented its 'parent' unit 216 Signal Squadron with a trophy in the form of a Golden Eagle.

Corporal Coxall, Sergeant Marsh and Staff Sergeant Nutter of 49th (West Riding) Signal Regiment (TA) in Bradford, c. 1963. National Servicemen often completed the balance of their reserve liability within the Territorial Army. Thus the TA enjoyed a considerable body of operational experience and skill. However, this asset was soon to diminish and a reappraisal of the TA's role had to be made leading to its reorganisation in 1967.

A mountain-top 'Radio Re-broadcast Site' with a Royal Naval Wessex Helicopter, Borneo. British forces deployed to Borneo in December 1962 and quickly suppressed an armed revolt in Brunei. However, continued terrorism sponsored by Indonesia called for reinforcement. 247 and 248 Gurkha Signal Squadrons supported both Gurkha and British units in the rugged jungle terrain. HF communications were difficult but ingenuity and determination were applied to build a successful VHF network of mountain top relay stations. Second Lieutenant (later General KCB CBE) Sam Cowan and his Gurkha soldiers, assisted in this dangerous task by skilled and courageous Royal Naval helicopter pilots, succeeded in inserting such a station on Mount Murud at 8,000 feet.

Joint Communications Centre, Borneo. In the early stages of the operation in Borneo communications were provided on a wasteful single service basis. The co-ordination of signal units was needed not only to provide efficiently manned Force communications but also a mobile reserve. Thus the Joint Communications Unit Borneo was formed in 1963. Static communications' centres manned by this unit were estab-lished at Joint Force Headquarters Labuan and at Headquarters 'West' Brigade at Kuching. The unit also provided a small air support communications network. By the end of the Indonesian confrontation over 3,000 officers and men had served in Signal units in Borneo and the operation was characterised by successful tri-service co-operation.

Captain B.F. Strange of 252 Signal Squadron leading a Security Patrol, Hong Kong, 1964. The Royal Signals Sailing Club Junk, the *Marie Stella* transported detachments of the Squadron to Lamma Island for patrols. Radio equipment was installed in the boat, enabling easy communication with HQ. The mountainous island had no roads or vehicles but the patrols were able to access most of the island by sailing around the coast and landing as near as possible to each of the villages.

Lieutenant (TOT) (later Lieutenant Colonel) Nigel Ribchester and Corporal Corless advise local workers after the floods in Hong Kong, 1966. During the early hours of the morning of 12 June 1966, Hong Kong experienced the heaviest rainfall since records began in 1840. The resulting chain of floods and landslides almost brought life in the Colony to a standstill. Communications were badly affected and the chief concern was the almost total loss of contact between Hong Kong and the New Territories. Men from HQ Royal Signals Hong Kong worked around the clock to restore the Colony to normal.

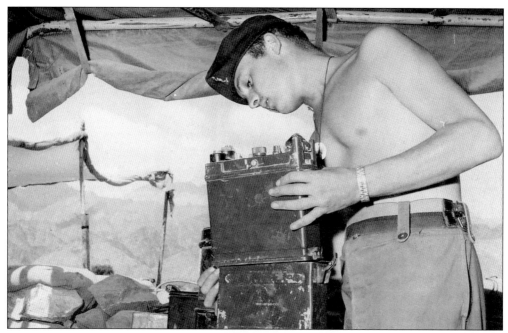

Radfan, 1963. In December 1963 operations were first mounted against Egyptian inspired rebels in the Radfan mountains, a tribal territory thirty miles north of Aden. These operations continued at various pitches of intensity until the British withdrawal from Aden in 1967. Communications were difficult and were focused on providing coverage of the main route between Aden and Dhala. Innovative approaches included the mounting of rebroadcast stations in RAF aircraft.

Officer Cadet (later Colonel) Michael Powell with Second Lieutenant (later Colonel and now Director of the Royal Signals Museum) Cliff Walters, Aden, 1966. Officer Cadet Powell was on attachment to 15th Signal Regiment in Aden during leave from the Royal Military Academy Sandhurst. On an expedition into the desert wastes around Beihan, on the edge of the infamous Empty Quarter, he was able to make radio contact with a party of other Sandhurst Cadets exercising in Ethiopia, over 1,000 miles away.

Line communications in Malta, 1965. Malta Signal Section, formed in 1923, replaced the Royal Engineers Signal Section. The Section became a Squadron during the Second World War and, from 1950 the communication facilities expanded further as Malta became a major NATO base. 235 Signal Squadron, established in 1954, operated the trunk system into the Commonwealth Communications Army Network (COMCAN). COMCAN linked the Ministry of Defence in London, via Droitwich, to stations in Canada, Kenya, Cyprus, Singapore and Malta. The network closed in 1968 as the Defence Communications Network took over strategic communications for all three Services. Royal Signals remained on the island until 1979.

601 Signal Troop (Ship) Gun Crew aboard HMS Meon, *1964.* 601 Troop, consisting of a Captain, a Yeoman of Signals and fifteen operators, was part of the Royal Naval Amphibious Warfare Squadron. Their function was to provide communications between the Headquarters Ship and headquarters ashore. Detachments went to sea in a variety of Squadron ships, from landing craft and assault ships to frigates. On board members of the Troop were regarded as part of the ship's company and, in addition to working alongside Naval communicators, performed other ship's duties including manning the guns.

Members of the Corps aboard HMS Hermes, 1966. As well as serving on ships, the Corps had affiliations with a number of HM vessels. HMS *Hermes* was the last Fleet Carrier and finished her operational service in the Falklands War. On a voyage to Gibraltar in 1966 the Royal Signals contingent was accorded a place of honour 'lining ship'.

Below: *Corporals Fred Stacey and Ron Stanton working on underground (UG) cable.* The Royal Signals was responsible for the provision of communications on all Royal Air Force airfields overseas. 21st Signal Regiment supported the Royal Air Force in Germany and maintained 500 kilometres of multi-pair UG cable, 2,600 telephone installations, 120 intercommunications systems and many other types of equipment providing the complicated and essential communications of the Strike airbases.

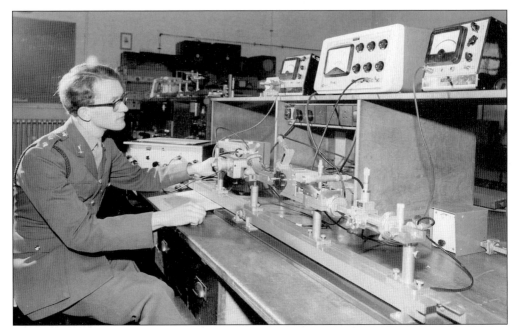

Lieutenant Rex (later Lieutenant Colonel) Stevenson reading for a BSc in Engineering at the Royal Military College of Science at Shrivenham, 1967. Technical qualifications have always been important to Royal Signals. Many officers have studied for first and second degrees at the Royal Military College of Science in Shrivenham enabling them to propose and develop pioneering technical solutions to operational communications' problems. RMCS will shortly cease to offer in-service degrees and future Service undergraduates will attend civilian universities.

A Terminal Equipment (TE) Technician Corporal lines up a Voice Frequency Telegraph Channel over a radio relay carrier system during a BRUIN exercise. The decision to field BRUIN was taken in 1964 but, by utilising existing equipment and 'off the shelf' tele-communications components, it was in service in BAOR by 1967. A key advantage of BRUIN was that, for the first time, the main radio transmitters could be separate from the headquarters thus reducing the chance of the HQ location being detected by the enemy.

A BRUIN 'COMCEN' moves into location in the snows of a German winter. The BRUIN Communications Centre (COMCEN) processed communications traffic, both voice and telegraph enabling headquarters to keep in touch with each other. They were sited on high ground and comprised radio relay vehicles and telephone exchanges. Two COMCENS were allocated to each division and four to the Corps area.

BRUIN Radio Relay equipment in a 'Fish Fryer'. One of the main radio relay equipments in use in BRUIN was the British C50. It was the first radio relay system to use a frequency synthesiser. The equipment was often mounted in vehicles but an airportable version was carried in trailers which had sloping lids not unlike those found on the fryers in fish and chip shops, hence the name 'Fish Fryer' Trailer.

Closed Circuit Television (CCTV), c. 1964. In 1962 the emerging technology of Close Circuit Television was tested to judge its effectiveness in supporting improved staff procedures at Corps Headquarters. An operational system was introduced in 1964 and was used predominantly to enable the Corps Commander to be updated from a distance by his staff branches. Taped recordings of the briefings were then flown by helicopter to subordinate headquarters.

Sergeants Smurthwaite and Smith, and Lance Corporals Williams and Myers, of 14th Signal Regiment, with the antenna dish of the first transportable satellite communications terminal. Satellite communications offered the opportunity for portable, secure, multi-channel links to be established to theatres of operation. These early satellite terminals were bulky and, although transportable, took a substantial crew several days to establish.

An Armoured Fighting Vehicle (AFV) 432. A new range of Armoured Fighting Vehicles was introduced in the 1960s to undertake a range of tasks including command and communications. They are still in service and have therefore been so for longer than the horse-drawn cable wagon. This particular AFV bears the name *Hermes* reflecting the link between the Corps and the fleet carrier.

CLANSMAN Radio. In the late 1950s Royal Signals planners, anticipating the use of computers to support command and control, planned the fielding of an integrated, networked communications system. A variety of projects was proposed but foundered through lack of funding or difficulties with international cooperation. However, part of the vision was realised with the introduction of the CLANSMAN range of radios in the early 1970s. At the time these radios were the most advanced in the world and they are still in service at every level of command throughout the whole Army.

The Colonel in Chief inspects the Guard of Honour, Freedom of Richmond Parade, 17 August 1964. The Colonel in Chief was accompanied by the Mayor of Richmond, Councillor R.W. Waldie OBE JP and preceded by Yeoman Warder G.A.E. Garvey, late Royal Signals. The Borough of Richmond accorded the Royal Signals the privilege of Freedom of the Town to cement the valued association, built up over nearly forty years, between the townspeople and the men and families of the Corps who were based in nearby Catterick.

The 50th Anniversary of the Battle of the Marne, Rheims, 1964. A contingent from 11th Signal Regiment and the Corps Band were granted the unique honour of taking part in a parade to commemorate the Battle of Marne in Rheims on 6 September 1964. President de Gaulle took the salute and as the Corps Guard of Honour, with swords drawn and bayonets fixed, approached the dais, the Band broke into 'It's a long way to Tipperary'. The delighted French crowd sang and whistled along with the tune and even the President smiled in appreciation of this well chosen number.

This Is Your Life, 1964. Eamonn Andrews with Captain Paul Burrough, Captain Jock Moss, Captain Stanley Bygrave, Major Eric Beaver, Captain Harry Bristow, RSM Feltham, and Signalman Drummond, members of 11th Indian Division Signals and all Prisoners of War of the Japanese. Sixteen years after the programme was broadcast, it emerged that Major Beaver and RSM Feltham had a fascinating story. Whilst prisoners they recorded in a diary details of 504 men of the Corps who died from disease, malnutrition or ill-treatment at the hands of the Japanese. Fearing discovery, the men buried their diary in a coffin marked 'Private Records'. The ruse was a success as the Japanese assumed this was just another British soldier being interred in the compound. The diary was later recovered and is now in the Corps Museum.

Brigadier (later Major General) A.J. Deane-Drummond DSO MC with Sergeant M.J. Blay, 3rd Signal Regiment at the National and Inter-Services Gliding Competition in 1964. Brigadier Deane-Drummond was National Gliding Champion in 1957. Commissioned into the Corps in 1937, he had a distinguished career. After serving with 3rd Division in the British Expeditionary Force, he volunteered for the first British parachute unit. When all members of the initial airborne operation in Italy were captured, he was the only one to escape. He served with Airborne Forces in North Africa and at Arnhem where he was again captured. However, by hiding in a cupboard for thirteen days, he managed to elude his captors. In post-war years he commanded the 3rd Division and later became Assistant Chief of the Defence Staff (Operations).

Admiral of the Fleet, Earl Mountbatten of Burma, accepts the Honorary Life Membership of the Royal Signals Association and Institution from Major General Michael Whistler on 5 February 1965. During his Naval career Lord Mountbatten had been a signaller and was instrumental in developing the art of naval signalling. When Chief of the Defence Staff, he was invited to accept the award as the world's most senior serving Communicator. Major General Whistler's appointment as Assistant Chief of the Defence Staff (Signals) was a new post created under Lord Mountbatten's influence, to provide central management for the communicators of all three Services.

WRAC leave 14th Signal Regiment, Boddington, 1965. In 1940 the women of the ATS arrived to run the Communcations Centre at Boddington. They continued their efficient performance of this task following the formation of the WRAC and after 14th Signal Regiment took over responsibilities for aspects of Defence Communications. The installation of the Telegraph Automatic Routing Equipment meant fewer operators were required and the WRAC were no longer needed. Thus, on 12 May 1965, they marched off parade for the last time.

Donald Campbell with members of the Corps, 1967. The Corps provided communications for Donald Campbell's ill-fated endeavour to break the world speed record on Coniston Water in 1967. Having set a new World Land Speed Record of 403.1mph at Lake Eyre in Australia, Donald Campbell then tried to become the first person to exceed 300mph on water. Sadly, he was killed in the attempt.

Major (later Lieutenant Colonel) Hugh Bonaker leads a detachment of the Corps from Buckingham Palace, 1972. The Corps performed Public Duties for the first time in September 1972 taking over the Queen's Guard from the Coldstream Guards.

Major General A.M.W. Whistler meets 'Laddie', 1964. During a Graduation Parade at the Junior Leaders' Regiment, the Regimental Band Mascot, 'Laddie' a large snowy white Pyrenean Mountain dog and his handler, Junior Signalman Fuller, were introduced to the General. The famous 'Ten Tors' Expedition which takes place in Devon each year was devised by a Royal Signals Officer, Lieutenant Colonel L.H.M. Gregory MBE when he was Commandant of the Junior Leaders' Regiment at Denbury in Devon.

Apprentice Radio Technician Brian Whitton, aged 18, working on D11/R234 radio equipment. The Army Apprentices' School was set up in Harrogate in 1947 and by the mid-1960s had become a College training only Royal Signals Apprentices. Savings measures under the 'Options for Change' plan forced its closure in 1996. This was a great loss to the Corps since the College provided a nurturing ground for more than half of all Foremen and Yeomen of Signals.

The new School of Signals in Blandford, 1960s. Following the decision to re-site the School of Signals, building to provide the necessary working and living accommodation commenced in 1964. The School was responsible for training all officers and for the professional development of senior NCOs and Warrant Officers. In August 1992 HM The Queen granted the School the Royal title.

The Royal Signals Trade Training School, Catterick. Officially opened by the Prime Minister on 24 September 1971, the new Trade Training School in Catterick was the latest in modern design and equipment. It could accommodate 1,000 students undertaking courses from basic trade training through to technical upgrading.

On a rooftop in Belfast, communicating via Wireless Set B70. Sectarian violence flared in Northern Ireland in 1969 in the wake of a movement to achieve equitable civil rights. The Army was deployed to keep the peace and, by the early 1970s, the deteriorating situation warranted a significant force including several Squadrons of the Corps. Communications were difficult and, before the introduction of specialised commercial networks, a variety of existing equipment was pressed into use. The B70 was a short range UHF radio relay system used in support of heavy anti-aircraft missile systems. It was used by 260 Signal Squadron which also deployed in the Infantry role.

Briefing the Brigade Commander's Rover Group. Given the sensitive nature of operations in the Province, it was vital that Brigade Commanders were always in touch with their Headquarters and with the situation on the ground. Royal Signals provided 'Rover Groups' consisting of two to three vehicles and, as well as manning the communications, provided security for the commander and key staff.

On a mobile patrol in Lurgan, 1974. General Peter Leng, GOC Northern Ireland, said of the Royal Signals that 'they were his most versatile soldiers. There was nothing they could not turn their hands to. They could march and shoot, they could patrol, they could defend and above all had provided him with technical skills and knowledge across the broadest possible canvas.' In the first twelve years of the troubles seven signallers lost their lives.

A Regimental Signals Officer, Northern Ireland 1971. In the 1970s some Royal Signals junior officers were attached to Battalions and Regiments of All Arms. They served as Troop Leaders or Platoon Commanders or, more rarely, as Regimental Signals Officers. These attachments, which varied in length from one to three years, were vital in ensuring the Corps retained a fundamental understanding of All Arms operations.

Corporal Gerry Jacques, Winner of the Queen's Medal at Bisley, 1973. With continuing operational commitments marksmanship remains a very necessary skill for signallers and the Corps has always maintained a high profile in the sport. The Queen's Medal is awarded to the winner of the Army Small Arms Championship at Bisley. In 1970 the Corps were clear winners of the Methuen Cup, a comprehensive test of battle shooting instituted by General The Lord Methuen whose descendent, the present Lord Methuen, served in Royal Signals.

Freedom on Lippstadt Parade, 1973. The Freedom of Lippstadt was granted to both 22nd Signal Regiment and the German Army Signal Battalion, 7th Fernmeldebatallion, in a unique joint ceremony in October 1973. The honour acknowledged the links forged between the Regiments and the Town and also the partnership that existed between the two units. By the mid 1970s at least 50% of the Corps was serving in BAOR which, following the effective end of Empire and the increasing tensions of the Cold War, had become the focus of the British Army's activity.

Six
From 1974 to 1989

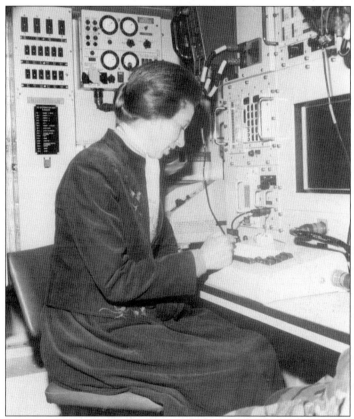

The Colonel in Chief operating PTARMIGAN, 1984. The mid-1980s heralded an era of revolution in battlefield communications. PTARMIGAN, introduced into service in 1984, was described as 'a quantum jump forward in tactical communications technology and in simplicity of use by the non-technical'. Working through a network of computer assisted centres, 'trunk nodes', it provides Divisional commanders with the ability to confer instantly with Brigade commanders in an environment totally secure from interception. It is more robust than earlier systems and, if one trunk node is knocked out, another automatically takes over. PTARMIGAN is still in service.

HM The Queen unveils a statue, Catterick, 10 July 1975. The statue, sculpted by Faith Winter, was commissioned to mark 50 years of the Corps in Catterick. Two Royal Signals soldiers are depicted wearing the uniforms and with equipment appropriate to the periods 1925 and 1975. When the Corps finally left Catterick in 1995, the statue was moved and now stands at the entrance to Blandford Camp.

Detachment of 6 Armoured Brigade HQ & Signal Squadron during a Patrol on the border between East and West Germany, 1975. In addition to training for the potential Soviet invasion of West Germany, Royal Signals units were required to participate in other operational security tasks such as guarding nuclear weapons' sites and patrolling the inner German border. These patrols were conducted in conjunction with the Bundesgrenzshutz (Federal Border Police) and the British Frontier Service.

Operation Burberry, 1977. In December 1977 the Army were called in to man military fire engines, the famous 'Green Goddesses', during the Firemen's strike. A number of Corps units undertook fire-fighting duties and, over the Christmas period, 8th Signal Regiment attended 183 incidents. In the aptly named 'Winter of Discontent' soldiers were also deployed to drive ambulances and were later put on stand-by when oil tanker drivers threatened industrial action.

The Queen reviews the Army in West Germany, 1977. On 7 July 1977, The Queen reviewed the Army at the Sennelager Training Area in West Germany as part of the celebrations to mark the Silver Jubilee of her reign. Most Royal Signals units based in Germany were involved in communications for the event and Lance Corporal (later Yeoman of Signals) Crilly of 7th Signal Regiment drove Major General Bagnall, General Officer Commanding 4th Division, in the vehicle following the Royal Range Rover.

Lieutenant Colonel Ian Sprackling with Major Mike Clowser Intelligence Corps, and Warrant Officer Class 1 (RSM) Robinson, 14th Signal Regiment (EW), 1977. The interception of enemy messages has always been a key factor of intelligence gathering. The inter-ception tool of the modern army is Electronic Warfare (EW). The effective use of EW by the Soviets in their invasion of Czechoslovakia and by the Americans in the Vietnam War prompted NATO to review its EW capability. It was decided that each National Corps should have a tactical EW capability and accordingly 14th Signal Regiment (EW) formed under the command of Lieutenant Colonel (later Major General and now Master of Signals) Ian Sprackling OBE in 1977.

The Colonel in Chief with members of 11th Signal Regiment, Catterick, 1978. On Wednesday 1 November 1978, HRH the Princess Anne made her first official visit to Royal Signals since being appointed Colonel in Chief of the Corps.

Erecting antennae, Cyprus 1978. Antennae are often large and complex structures, requiring help from outside agencies to erect them safely. Corporal Allen and Lance Corporal Morgan of 254 (United Nations) Signal Squadron, assisted by Major C. Blount, Army Air Corps, in a Sioux helicopter, are shown fitting a log periodic antenna on a seventy-foot mast at Salt Lake Camp, Larnaca, the home of the Swedish Contingent to the UN Forces in Cyprus.

Lieutenant Jim Barrie of 249 Signal Squadron AMF(L), 1980. 249 Signal Squadron is a part of the British contingent of the multi-national Reserve of the Supreme Allied Commander Europe, the ACE Mobile Force (AMF). This radio squadron operates in the Arctic and on the Southern flank in Turkey. All members are, therefore, trained to work in both extremes of climate. Lieutenant Barrie was subsequently attached to 2 Para in the Falklands War and was killed at the battle of Goose Green in 1982.

Lieutenant Jane Sugden with Royal Signals, 1980. From the mid 1970s a number of WRAC were given the opportunity to become permanently employed by Royal Signals and fulfilled many of the same tasks as their male counterparts. Lieutenant (later Captain Stockdale) Jane Sugden became the first female officer to command a troop of male soldiers. Following the disbandment of the WRAC in 1992, women were able to join the Royal Signals and wear the Corps cap badge. The name of private soldiers was then changed from 'Signalman' to 'Signaller'.

Corporal McKenzie of 8 Field Force, Zimbabwe, 1980. The Corps formed 15% of a Commonwealth force deployed to monitor the elections and a cease-fire between the Government forces of Ian Smith and guerrilla groups prior to the creation of the Republic of Zimbabwe in 1980. Code named Agila, the operation provided the first opportunity to test the CLANSMAN Combat Net Radio under active service conditions. The system worked admirably and proved very reliable.

Signalman N.J. Humphries, of 30th Signal Regiment, brings in a RAF Puma at Karoi, during Operation Agila.

The Falklands War, Racal Tactical Satellite Communications dish (TACSATCOM) at Ajax Bay with Argentinian prisoners in the background, 1982. On 5 April 1982, the Prime Minister, Margaret Thatcher, ordered the Task Force to set sail for the Falkland Islands to liberate the islands from the invading Argentinian forces. Six hundred men of the Royal Signals took part in the eighty-nine days of war that followed. Members of 30th Signal Regiment, 5 Infantry Brigade HQ and Signal Squadron and 244 Signal Squadron took part in the land battles and Signal detachments provided rear links for 2 and 3 Para, 2 Scots Guards, 1 Welsh Guards, 1/7 Gurkha Rifles and the Special Boat Service. The new Racal TACSATCOM provided the strategic contingency rear link communications to the United Kingdom throughout the war.

Major Mike Forge. 5 Infantry Brigade landed at San Carlos on 1 June 1982. Major Mike Forge, Officer Commanding the Brigade Signal Squadron, and Staff Sergeant Joe Baker flew in a Gazelle of 656 Squadron Army Air Corps to check the communication link to 2 Para at Fitzroy. The helicopter was shot down and all on board were killed.

TRIFFID equipment being winched into position by a Sea King helicopter, The Falklands. TRIFFID, a microwave radio relay system, later to become part of PTARMIGAN was deployed in the Falklands. At the end of the fighting, when most communications facilities on the Islands had been damaged or destroyed, TRIFFID was used to link outlying communities, isolated British troops and the advance early warning radar sites.

Lieutenant Colonel (later Colonel) Roger Thompson with a captured Argentinean Oelikon Gun. Lieutenant Colonel Thompson commanded 30th Signal Regiment during the Falklands campaign. Since the war the Corps has continuously contributed a substantial number of soldiers to the maintenance of communications on the Islands.

The Blue Helmets Freefall Parachute Team, 1983. The Team was formed by Captain Mike Forge in 1973. Although the Blue Helmets represented the Corps and the British Army at public and service events worldwide, its primary task was to co-ordinate freefall parachuting within the Corps and to foster interest in the sport. In the early 1990s the Team was disbanded but reformed in 2002.

Farewell to the Fijians, 1983. In 1961 200 Fijians were recruited into the British Army and twenty-nine joined the Corps. 1983 marked the twenty-two-year point in their careers and a Parade was held to bid them farewell. Their contribution, both at work and at play, was always of the highest order and their skills on the rugby field will be remembered for many years. Happily, the Corps is once again recruiting from the island of Fiji.

The Army Apprentices' College Canoe Team with trophies won during the 1983 season. Sport was a key part of the curriculum at the College fostering teamwork and physical fitness. Canoeing was particularly important as an adventurous training pursuit but apprentices excelled at most sports and competed at both Junior and Army levels and for the County of Yorkshire.

Chief Yeoman Warder W. Russell and Yeoman Gaoler A. Copestake, The Tower of London, 1984. Retired Warrant Officers and Staff Sergeants of the Army and the Royal Air Force are eligible to become Yeoman Warders of the Tower of London. A high proportion of Warders are retired members of the Corps and, at the time of writing, the Chief Yeoman Warder and the Yeoman Gaoler are again both Royal Signals.

10th Signal Regiment on Public Duties, 1984. In April 1984, 2 Squadron was tasked with providing communications for the State Visit of His Royal Highness The Emir of Bahrein. Radio links had to be provided from Heathrow to Windsor and from Windsor to London. Captain Nigel Moore and Signalman Kevin Cunningham took advantage of the 'height gain' of the Round Tower at Windsor Castle.

Lieutenant Colonel (later Colonel) Mike Ayrton receives a framed scroll from Air Marshall Sir Patrick Hine, 1984. In recognition of the support given by 21st Signal Regiment (Air Support) to the Royal Air Force it was granted the unique honour and privilege of displaying the RAF Germany Badge on its Regimental flag and insignia. The presentation was made at a parade marking the Silver Jubilee of the Regiment.

Signalman Voros on Plessey Douglas, 1984. The Corps, assisted by sponsorship from the Plessey Company, purchased a bay Hannoverian gelding to promote interest in the sport of competitive riding. Pictured with Signalman Voros are Lieutenant Colonel J.H. Fisher, the Master of Signals, Major General J.M.W. Badcock and Lieutenant (later Captain) Suzy Reed, WRAC.

Lieutenant Mark Campbell and Sergeant Jack Dempsey, Beirut, 1983. A British contingent, which included about sixty members of the Corps, contributed to a Multi-National peacekeeping force in Beirut in late 1983. The ceasefire that had been brokered between the warring factions, the Moslems and Christians, was shaky and by February of 1984 the situation became so dangerous that the Force had to be withdrawn.

PTARMIGAN Parade, Blandford, 1984. On 14 December 1984 the first PTARMIGAN installations left Blandford for Verden in West Germany. A parade was held to mark this historic occasion and the picture shows Captain (later Lieutenant Colonel MBE) Miles Stockdale, the Convoy Commander, requesting permission to depart from Brigadier John Almonds, Commander School of Signals.

The Project WAVELL Implementation Team, 1977. Royal Signals was at the forefront of development in the application of computing technology to the battlefield. The decreasing size of computers coupled with greater capability offered the possibility of considerably enhanced methods of handling battlefield information. WAVELL, introduced into service alongside PTARMIGAN in 1985, was the first battlefield Command and Control Information System.

PTARMIGAN, mobile use of 'single channel' radio access – the military mobile 'phone. Investment by the Ministry of Defence in new technology for PTARMIGAN had a significant impact on the civilian telecommunications world. PTARMIGAN's switching technology provided a basis for the modern BT network and its approach to mobile communications influenced the development of the mobile phone.

Brigadier (later General KCB CBE ADC Gen) Sam Cowan, visiting 3rd Armoured Division HQ & Signal Regiment on exercise in Germany, 1985. As Commander Communications 1st British Corps, Brigadier Cowan was instrumental in the successful fielding of PTARMIGAN and WAVELL.

The White Helmets Motorcycle Display Team with Roy Castle, 1986. The descendents of the early Royal Signals Display Team continue to enthral audiences with their thrilling and skilful exploits. The team currently hold the World Record for the largest, unsupported human pyramid of fifty-two riders on eight machines. Roy Castle joined thirty-five team members, again on eight bikes, for the children's television series *Record Breakers* in 1986. World Motorcycle Champion Geoff Duke is one of many past members of the team who have became famous in the world of competitive riding.

Caron Keating with families of 201 Signal Squadron, Blue Peter Appeal 1987. Fund raising and the support of charities have always featured in the Corps activities. The Bring and Buy Sale organised by the families of 201 Signal Squadron in Hohne, West Germany raised £3,000 for the Blue Peter Sight Savers Appeal.

Staff Sergeant Don Chester passing a Canadian Coastguard ship, Exercise Silver Orca, 1987. Staff Sergeant Chester was part of a five-man team that attempted to canoe 1,000 kilometres of largely uninhabited coastline off Vancouver Island. Gale force winds and a bout of food poisoning meant that only 500 kilometres was completed but the exercise proved demanding as well as instructive and tested both physical and mental endurance.

The Duchess of Kent presents the Army Challenge Cup to Sergeant Sandy Brown, 1988. The School of Signals beat 28th Amphibious Engineer Regiment to win the Army Challenge Cup in the centenary year of the competition in 1988. The Corps, with a long tradition of soccer success, has won the Cup on a number of occasions. Many famous footballers have served with Royal Signals, including Gordon Banks.

The Prime Minister and Mr Dennis Thatcher with Lieutenant (later Captain) Phillippa Owens MBE, Namibia 1989. The United Nations deployed a force to Namibia in 1989 to monitor its transition to independence. 30th Signal Regiment was tasked with providing communications for the UN Transitional Assistance Group. The unit's communications and, in the early stages, its prompt and resourceful action played a major role in ensuring that free and fair elections were able to take place.

WOI RSM (later Major) Rab Young, Staff Sergeant (Foreman of Signals) Kassim and colleagues of The Berlin Signal Regiment with East German Border Guards, Berlin 1989. The crumbling of the infamous wall dividing Berlin enabled adversaries, who had faced each other across the divide for over forty years, to meet at last in friendship. Soldiers and families of the Berlin Signal Regiment joined thousands of runners from all over Europe to take part in the first East/West Fun Run. Military competitors were able to cross into the East through the Brandenburg Gate rather than via the old 'Checkpoint Charlie'. The ending of the Cold War resulted in reorganisation and a reduction in the size of the Corps in Germany.

Seven
From 1990 to 2002

The Gulf War 1990-1991. In the latter half of 1990, when politicians were debating 'peace dividend' troop reductions, a major threat developed in the Middle East with the Iraqi invasion of Kuwait. As always, elements of the Corps were first into theatre and some eight months later were the last to leave. At the height of the War over 2,000 members of Royal Signals were deployed carrying out the full range of their operational tasks from electronic warfare, radio and satellite communication to support for Special Forces. PTARMIGAN was given its baptism of fire in the conflict and soon proved its worth forming an unbroken chain of communications from Dharan on the coast to 7th Corps Headquarters and west into the Divisional Tactical Assembly Area, a distance of 540 kilometres.

Operational Systems Command (OSC) 131, 1 Squadron 1st Armoured Division HQ and Signal Regiment. First into Iraq and the first operational OSC in the Gulf. From left to right, front row: WOII (later WOI) (Yeoman of Signals) Purvis, Lance Corporal (later Yeoman of Signals) Jackson and WOII (Squadron Sergeant Major) Bragg. Back row: Major Whittaker, Captain (later Major) Summerville, Staff Sergeant (Yeoman of Signals) Haresign and Sergeant (later Yeoman of Signals) Dennis. Royal Signals personnel were not only first into Iraq but also captured the first Iraqi prisoners in the ground war.

Sergeant (later WOI CRSM) Sean Keilty and Corporal John O'Donnell on the Basra Road, Iraq, 1991. In the aftermath of the Gulf War, Sergeant Keilty and Corporal O'Donnell of 22nd Signal Regiment spent four months based in 'Black Adder' Camp on attachment to the Royal Pioneer Corps. Their grim task was to help with the burial of casualties from the war.

Staff Sergeant (later Captain) Steve Smoothy, Bosnia, 1993. After the collapse of communism in Yugoslavia ethnic groups in the Federation sought self-determination. Resistance by the Serb dominated central Government led to inter-communal violence and ethnic cleansing. The international community sent in monitors, including Corps personnel, but civil war erupted and the United Nations deployed a Protection Force (UNPROFOR) to protect thousands of refugees. 211 Signal Squadron, commanded by Major (later Colonel) Don Steele, moved into the region at ten days' notice. Signal Squadrons continued to support UNPROFOR until the signing of the Dayton Peace Accord.

Corporal Lawrence sets up a Satellite Communications Dish in Angola, 1995. The United Nations Angola Verification Mission was set up in 1995 to oversee the cease-fire and demobilisation of the rebel forces in Angola. 30th Signal Regiment was tasked with providing communications for the mission and deployed with 9th Regiment Royal Logistic Corps.

3rd Division Reunion Club Veterans, Caen 1994. Fifty years on from the D-Day landings, Veterans of 3rd Infantry Division returned to Normandy for a programme of events in La Breche, Hermanville, Bayeux and Arromanches. The Mayor of Caen presented the Veterans with D-Day Commemorative Medals on behalf of a grateful France.

The Colonel in Chief with members of the Corps, Blandford 1995. The Colonel in Chief visited Blandford on 9 July 1995 during celebrations to mark the 75th Anniversary of the Corps. A highlight of her programme was the opening of the new extension to the Royal Signals Museum.

Lance Corporal Mears with Mr Rick Gainsborough-Foot OBE, the Master Elect of the Worshipful Company of Information Technologists, and the Master of Signals (Major General Archie Birtwistle) at the Mansion House, 1995. Lance Corporal Mears of the Army Apprentices' College was the first winner of the IT Apprentice of the Year award instigated by the Worshipful Company of Information Technologists to mark the 75th Anniversary of the Corps.

Cross Country Champion, Signaller Sharon Elder, May 1995. Signaller Elder won the SE District Cross Country Championships, the London District Cross Country title, the Army 3,000m and also competed at international level. From the earliest days of the Corps signallers have continued to excel in athletics and produce world-class exponents of the sport, including Staff Sergeant Callendar and Kriss Akabusi.

Return to Maresfield, October 1995. A remarkable achievement of the 75th Anniversary year was the amazing journey undertaken by eighty-year-old Major Ted Hughes. He planned to ride 600 miles, retracing the moves of the Corps from Maresfield, Sussex to Catterick, Yorkshire and Blandford in Dorset. He is pictured at Maresfield in the uniform of the Middlesex Yeomanry with Major General Hellier, Mrs Pegg, Chairman of Maresfield Parish Council, Councillor Reg Gray, Mayor of Uckfield and Corporal Downie of the Middlesex Yeomanry. On the next 'leg' of the journey Major Hughes was taken ill and sadly died a few weeks later.

The Corps Band march past Clarence House, 1995. The Corps undertook Public Duties in its 75th anniversary year and the Band played at Clarence House for The Queen Mother's birthday. The Band is widely acknowledged to be one of the best in the Army. Its strength has fluctuated over the years from over 130 musicians in post-war days to the current level of thirty-five. Corps music has also long been provided by the very competent Band of 34th Signal Regiment (V) and the Corps' Pipes and Drums with pipers and drummers drawn from both Territorial and Regular Signal units.

Line Training Facilities at Blandford, 1996. In 1996 when Royal Signals Trade Training was transferred from its purpose built accommodation in Catterick to Blandford, rapid expansion of the School of Signals was necessary in order to minimise disruption to training. 81 Signal Squadron (V) built new line training facilities and installed local computer networks.

Sergeant Peter Curtis receives The Army Rugby Cup on behalf of 2nd Signal Regiment, 1997. In 1997 Royal Signals won both the Major and Minor Unit titles in the Army Rugby Cup. 2nd Signal Regiment had a comfortable victory beating Royal Welsh Fusiliers 31 to 11 and 216 Signal Squadron beat 29th Regiment RLC. The Corps has produced some seventeen International players and, in National Service days, could take on and defeat first class clubs. 7th Signal Regiment entered the Guinness Book of Records in 1980 with a score of 184 to nil in an Army Cup match.

Signaller Mike Dyer, son of the late Major Dickie Dyer MBE R Signals, 212 Signal Squadron, Bosnia. The Accord negotiated at the Dayton Peace Talks stabilised the Bosnian Civil War and the Allied Rapid Reaction Corps (ARRC) deployed as the Intervention Force (IFOR) to implement its provisions. The communications elements of the force included the whole of 1st Signal Brigade as well as 1st Armoured Division Signal Regiment.

Lieutenant Colonel David Jones, Commanding Officer, 7th Signal Regiment, Kosovo, 1999. The Balkans conflict spilled over into the Serbian province of Kosovo in 1999 where the majority Albanians sought independence. NATO intervened and the ARRC was again called upon to help calm the situation, this time as 'Kosovo Force' (KFOR). This operation saw the largest mobilisation of British forces since the Gulf War with a significant contribution drawn from most Royal Signals units. KFOR is still in place but the Corps' contribution has been reduced to a Squadron.

Signaller Simon Shepherd rescues a young girl during floods in York, 2000. In the autumn and winter of 2000 severe flooding affected the City of York. Early in November 2nd Signal Regiment was called in to help. For many days, without a break, members of the Regiment filled sandbags and moved people and their possessions to safety. In January 2001, in recognition of their efforts, the Regiment was awarded Freedom of the City.

The John Laing *leaves Portsmouth at the start of the British Army Antarctic Expedition (BAAE), 27 August 2001.* Echoing in the footsteps of Smijth-Windham, Thompson and Meikeljohn, Royal Signals made a major contribution to the BAAE. The crews on the first two legs of the *John Laing*'s journey to the Antarctic were all members of the Corps. The Skipper, Lieutenant Colonel Andy Bristow, was one of the joint leaders of the expedition and Major Jim Wood the expedition's scientist. The aim of the expedition was to explore the Danco Coast of Antarctica by ski and sail to record historical, wildlife and geographical information.

Signaller Monk of 97 Signal Squadron (V), the Metal Factory, Banja Luka, Bosnia, 2002. The deployment of the Invention Force (IFOR) in Bosnia stabilised the situation sufficiently to allow for a reduction of force levels. However, there is an enduring commitment to peace-keeping in the region which involves a significant proportion of signallers. November 2001 saw the first use of a formed Territorial Army Signal Squadron, all voluntarily mobilised as 97 Signal Squadron (V).

Major Neil Fraser and Captain Karl Jeeves, Afghanistan, 2002. Following the terrorist outrages of 11 September 2001, members of the Corps are once again at the forefront of the high profile operation in Afghanistan. Elements of 3 (UK) Divisional Signal Regiment and 16 Air Assault Brigade carry on the traditions of their Sapper ancestors who were also called to serve in far-flung corners of the world. In the 130-year history of signalling, starting with 'C' Telegraph Troop Royal Engineers, technical advances have fundamentally altered methods of battlefield communication but the requirements demanded of signallers, determination, professionalism and military skills will never change.